HALF-TRUTH IN SENTENCING

A New Look at America's Century-Old Drug Policy

Daniel M. Rouleau, J.D.

TABLE OF CONTENTS

I. Introduction

> "America's public enemy number one in the United States is drug abuse. In order to fight and defeat this enemy, it is necessary to wage a new, all-out offensive."[1]

The use of intoxicating substances has been a political, legal, and social point of contention in America since the beginning of the twentieth century, inspiring constitutional amendments and scores of federal laws. Despite the rise and fall of the constitutional prohibition of alcohol, the prohibition of other intoxicants has remained in effect. Alcohol has a prominent place in American culture, from corporate happy hours to wedding champagne toasts, while other intoxicants associated culturally with non-white ethnic populations are outlawed with severe penalties for their possession, sale, or manufacture. Drug offenders encounter unique consequences that are never fully enumerated in the courtroom during sentencing. Additional consequences stem from federal and state-level policies that vary across the nation.

This book will first examine the rise of punitive prohibition in federal drug policy, highlighting key federal legislation passed in

---

[1] President Richard Nixon, Remarks About an Intensified Program for Drug Abuse Prevention and Control at the White House Briefing Room (June 17, 1971) (online by Gerhard Peters and John T. Woolley, *The American Presidency Project*. http://www.presidency.ucsb.edu/ws/?pid=3047).

the attempt to quell the use of intoxicating substances in the United States. The second section will focus on heroin and opiates, which should be the key topic of concern in America's drug policy. Third, several major collateral consequences stemming from drug offenses will be examined, including federal, state, and mixed responsibility consequences. Last, solutions are proposed to mitigate the collateral consequences of drug offenses and reduce the long-term impacts that serve as significant barriers to citizen reintegration into society following an encounter with the criminal justice system.

Every year, millions of Americans are effected by state and federal drug policies. Although this is framed most often as a criminal justice issue, drug policy has tangential effects in prison populations, mental health treatment, medical options, domestic relations, economy, and even the day-to-day lives of a variety of American communities where drug use is increasing, and increasingly devastating.

A cardinal point of American politics: no one gets elected by looking "soft on crime." However, the era of avoiding discussions of American drug policy in a meaningful manner is over. With so many Americans who have used illegal drugs, been incarcerated for them, or had families torn apart by overdose, incarceration, or violence, the time for serious conversation of the effectiveness of current American drug policies is overdue. Without serious reform to federal and state drug policies, increasingly large sections of American communities will suffer under the current system of punitive prohibition. Hopefully, this book can be a wake-up call to those who are unaware of the way our system is currently structured, and prompt reform to a results-oriented system that allows individuals effected by drug convictions to reintegrate back into society as productive citizens.

The inspiration for this book comes from personal interactions with the criminal justice system resulting from Virginia's outdated drug policies and seeing first-hand the death and destruction caused by addictive, deadly drugs. Friends have died using legal and illegal drugs. Others have resorted to criminal activities or accepting employment far below their skill and ability merely because of a single criminal justice interaction that forever branded them with the title of "drug offender" or "felon." The hope is that this book will further the discussion about effective criminal justice policies, and how freedom-loving people should address America's drug policy.

II.   The History of American Punitive Prohibition

1.   1800 – 1900

Prior to the twentieth century, opium products were commonly used across the United States. So common, in fact, that large international opium imports were required to satisfy the demand, particularly in the Northeastern United States.[2] These products were generally unregulated, available commercially in mixtures or by prescription from doctors or pharmacists. Doctors maintained narcotic addicts, and they themselves comprised the largest group of male addicts. Overall, however, women comprised the largest group of opium users. Opiate addiction among the general population increased following the Civil war, and society began to take notice of the seriousness of opiate addiction, sometimes called "soldier's disease."[3]

In 1884, cocaine was introduced, and was quickly incorporated into the variety of unregulated drug cocktails available at any local pharmacy. Cocaine became socially popular, and was available in medicinal mixtures, fountain sodas, and the

---

[2] John P. Hoffman, *The Historical Shift in the Perception of Opiates: From Medicine to Social Menace.* 22 J. OF PSYCHOACTIVE DRUGS, no. 1, Jan. 1990, at 53, 56.
[3] *Id.* at 57.

popular wine-based drink, Vin Mariana.[4] Public sentiment began to change regarding the availability of intoxicating substances with the increasing racial diversity in society following the Civil War, particularly in the South.[5]

2.   1900 – 1930

At the turn of the twentieth century, there were approximately a quarter million narcotic addicts, out of the United States population of 76 million.[6] Prior to 1906, there were approximately 50,000 "patent medicines," which contained a variety of substances and claimed to cure nearly everything from baldness to cancer. The patent medicine industry was worth an estimated $2 billion in 2016 value.[7] State laws regulated the sale of Patent Medicines, but there was a concentrated effort by pharmaceutical companies to lobby against any federal legislation.[8] The first major federal law regulating consumable

---

[4] DORIS MARIE PROVINE, UNEQUAL UNDER LAW: RACE IN THE WAR ON DRUGS 65–66 (2007).
[5] Peter J. Boettke, et al., Article, *Keep Off the Grass: The Economics of Prohibition and U.S. Drug Policy*, 91 OR. L. REV. 1069, 1073 (2013).
[6] Eric E. Sterling, Symposium, *The Sentencing Controversy: Punishment and Policy In The War Against Drugs: The Sentencing Boomerang: Drug Prohibition Politics And Reform*, 40 VILL. L. REV. 383, 392.
[7] JAMES HARVEY YOUNG, THE TOADSTOOL MILLIONAIRES: A SOCIAL HISTORY OF PATENT MEDICINES IN AMERICA BEFORE FEDERAL REGULATION 93–110; 226–45 (1961).
[8] Russel S. Sobel, *Public Health and The Placebo: The Legacy of the 1906 Pure Food and Drug Act.* 21 CATO JOURNAL, no. 3, Winter 2002, at 463, 468.

substances was the Pure Food and Drug Act of 1906.[9] The law aimed to aid consumers in making informed decision by imposing labeling requirements on the producers of consumables, but placed no restrictions on the substances themselves if clearly and correctly labeled.[10]

In the view of the U.S. government, the permissive federal stance "unwittingly encouraged" use of opium and morphine "to the great detriment of Chinese immigrants and . . . not only the criminal and defective classes, but of higher ranks of society."[11] "Cocaine . . . has proved to be a creator of criminals and of unusual forms of violence and has been a potent incentive in driving the primitive classes of the community all over the country to abnormal crimes."[12] The first federal law that prohibited unlicensed sale, distribution, and possession of opium and cocaine products within the United States was the 1914 Harrison Act. Earlier legislation had restricted the importation of opium; this act implemented federal control over the importation, manufacture, and distribution of narcotics in interstate commerce. The act

---

[9] Pure Food and Drug Act of 1906, Pub. L. No 59-381, 34 Stat. 768 (1906).
[10] DRUG COMPOUNDING: BACKGROUND, ISSUES AND FDA OVERSIGHT 45 (Martti Bram ed., 2014).
[11] S. DOC. NO. 61–377, at 2 (2d Sess. 1910).
[12] *Id.*

required the payment of a special tax, and only medical professionals, patients properly prescribed these substances, and government agents could possess these drugs legally.[13] Violation of this law was punished by a fine up to $2,000[14], equivalent to nearly $50,000 in 2017 currency, imprisonment for up to 5 years, or both.[15]

In 1919, the era formally known as Prohibition began with the ratification of the Eighteenth Amendment to the U.S. Constitution.[16] The Eighteenth amendment and the Volstead Act made the production, sale, and importation of alcoholic beverages illegal. Prohibition led to a drastic increase in organized crime and corruption to supply the demand for alcohol still present in the American public. The notorious rise of Al Capone and his criminal empire of Chicago happened concurrent to the enforcement of prohibition.[17] During this time, treasury agents continued to enforce the Harrison Act against users and illegal sellers of opium and cocaine, as well as doctors who prescribed these substances to maintain addicts. The Supreme Court upheld the constitutionality

---

[13] Harrison Act of 1914, Pub. L. No. 63-223, 38 Stat. 785, §§1-2 (1914).
[14] $2,000 (1914) is approximately $47,000 (2017) accounting for inflation. Dollartimes.com
[15] *Id.* at § 9.
[16] U.S. CONST. amend. XVIII.
[17] EDWARD D. SULLIVAN, RATTLING THE CUP ON CHICAGO CRIME 1929.

of the Harrison Act and convictions of doctors prescribing narcotics to addicts.[18]

3.   1930 – 1960

The formal era of Prohibition ended in 1933 with the ratification of the Twenty-First Amendment that repealed the Eighteenth Amendment and alcohol legally reentered the market. The prohibitive stances on other intoxicating substances remained, and punitive policies continued to expand in scope and severity. A key proponent of the punitive prohibition of narcotics, and the expansion of such policies, was Harry Anslinger, the Commissioner of the Bureau of Narcotics, a subdivision of the treasury department. Anslinger used racism and prejudice against Blacks, Hispanics, and Asians to push a law targeting marihuana,[19] framing it in a congressional hearing as inherently dangerous with

---

[18] *See, e.g.*, United States v. Doremus, 249 U.S. 86 (1919) (upholding Harrison Act as Constitutional under U.S. Const. art. I, § 8); Jin Fuey Moy v. United States, 254 U.S. 189 (1920) (Applying immunity from the Harrison Act only when operating "in the course of his professional duty," which cannot include maintaining addicts).

[19] RUDOLPH J. GERBER, LEGALIZING MARIJUANA: DRUG POLICY REFORM AND PROHIBITION POLITICS PP. 9 (2004) ("There are 100,000 total marijuana smokers in the US, and most are Negroes, Hispanics, Filipinos and entertainers. Their Satanic music, jazz and swing, result from marijuana usage. This marijuana causes white women to seek sexual relations with Negroes, entertainers, and any others.").

reports of marijuana-induced insanity and atrocious violence.[20] Congressional reports highlighted marijuana pushed on "high-school children . . . by unscrupulous peddlers" and use by "hardened criminals."[21] The Marihuana Tax Act of 1937 was another drug-targeted tax act that required special taxes from manufactures, importers, and researchers of marijuana. Despite the name, the primarily purpose was to restricted access to marijuana for illicit uses across the United States.[22] Like the Harrison Act, the law also placed heavy criminal sanctions on users and sellers who did not comply with the Marihuana tax act.[23]

By 1940, marijuana, cocaine, and most forms of opium were federally prohibited. Despite complete prohibition, Illegal drug use continued, although trafficking in illegal substances was curbed by the world-wide conflict of World War II.[24] Following the Second World War, the U.S. enacted laws with longer, more

---

[20] *Taxation of Marihuana: Hearings on H.R. 6385 Before the H. Comm. On Ways and Means*, 75th Cong. 21–23 (1937) (statement of Harry Anslinger, Commissioner of Narcotics, Bureau of Narcotics, Department of the Treasury).

[21] H.R. Rep. No. 75-792 at 2–3 (1937).

[22] Marihuana Tax Act of 1937, Pub. L. No. 75-238, §§ 1–2, 50 Stat. 551, 551–52 (1937).

[23] Pub. L. No. 75-238, § 12, 50 Stat. 551, 556 (1937).

[24] *NARCOTICS TRAFFIC IS CURBED BY WAR; League of Nations Section in Report Stresses Breach in Communications POST-WAR CONTROL URGED Problems in Legitimate Use of 'Dangerous Drugs' Due to War Also Outlined.* N.Y. TIMES, September 27, 1942 (available at http://query.nytimes.com/gst/abstract.html?res=990CEFDC1F3CE33BBC4F51D FBF668389659EDE&legacy=true#).

severe punishments for possession and sale of narcotics to squelch the perceived threat to society posed by criminal drug users. In 1951, a new amendment to federal drug laws created the first mandatory minimum drug sentence, requiring no less than 2 years for first-offense sale of narcotics.[25] The Narcotic Control Act of 1956 allowed juries to impose a death sentence for a conviction of selling heroin to a minor.[26] The harsh drug policy during this time cemented punitive prohibition in American politics, driven largely by socioeconomic and ethnic stereotypes first enumerated by Anslinger.

4. <u>1960 – 1980</u>

Only four million Americans had experimented with illegal drugs by 1960, but popular tolerance of drug use in this era altered the landscape of America forever.[27] Social scientists examined drug use, interestingly finding that most drug users studied were "legitimate people" who maintained regular employment despite addiction to a narcotic drug.[28] American

---

[25] Pub. L. 82-255, § 2, 65 Stat. 767, 768 (1951) ("An Act to amend the penalty provisions applicable to persons convicted of violating certain narcotic laws, and for other purposes.").

[26] Narcotic Control Act of 1956, Pub. L. 84-728, § 107, 70 stat. 567, 571 (1956).

[27] DRUG ENFORCEMENT ADMINISTRATION, *1970–75*, 4 https://www.dea.gov/about/history/1970-1975.pdf.

[28] Charles Winick, *Social Behavior, Public Policy, and Nonharmful Drug Use*, 69 THE MILBANK Q., no. 3, 1991, at 437, 439.

policy towards drugs remained punitive with the increased perception of drug use. The principal purpose of the Comprehensive Drug Abuse Prevention and Control Act of 1970 was "to deal in a comprehensive fashion with the growing menace of drug abuse in the United States."[29] The Act codified the drug schedules still used today to classify controlled substances, and revised the criminal penalties for federal drug offenses, removing some of the draconian penalties from 1950's federal drug legislation.[30]

President Nixon stepped up drug interdiction efforts in the United States by declaring "an all-out global war on the drug menace" and defined the drug policy across the United States for the next 30 years. Federal drug enforcement was divided among multiple agencies, so President Nixon issued an executive order in 1973that collated federal drug law enforcement into a single mega-agency: The Drug Enforcement Administration ("DEA").[31] When the DEA was formed, the agency had 1,470 agents with a budget of $74.9 million. [32]

---

[29] H.R. Rpt. 91-1444, at 1 (1970).
[30] Comprehensive Drug Abuse Prevention and Control Act of 1970, Pub. L. 91-513, § 202, 84 Stat. 1236, 1247 (1970).
[31] 38 F.R. 18357 (1973).
[32] DRUG ENFORCEMENT ADMINISTRATION, *1970–75*, 4. https://www.dea.gov/about/history/1970-1975.pdf.

5.   1980 – 2000

The most intense phase of drug enforcement occurred during the 1980's, resulting in the United States' extraordinary increase in its incarcerated population, now highest in the world.[33] In 1980, there were approximately 40,900 individuals in American jails and prisons for drug charges.[34] Prior to the 1985 emergence of "crack cocaine," many major cities police departments had begun to crack down on "drug bazaars" and open street drug dealing. In New York City, police sweeps resulted in thousands of street dealers of heroin and powdered cocaine being arrested.[35] The imposition of decades long sentences for non-violent drug crimes was affirmed by the Supreme Court, holding the 8th amendment does not allow federal courts to determine the appropriateness of sentences established by state legislatures.[36]

---

[33] Adam Liptak, *U.S. prison population dwarfs that of other nations*. N.Y. TIMES, April 23, 2008 (available at http://www.nytimes.com/2008/04/23/world/americas/23iht-23prison.12253738.html) ("The United States has less than 5 percent of the world's population. But it has almost a quarter of the world's prisoners.")

[34] The Sentencing Project, Trends in Corrections Fact Sheet, 3 http://sentencingproject.org/doc/publications/inc_Trends_in_Corrections_Fact_sheet.pdf.

[35] MATTHEW B. ROBINSON & RENEE G. SCHERLEN, LIES, DAMNED LIES, AND DRUG WAR STATISTICS: A CRITICAL ANALYSIS OF CLAIMS MADE BY THE OFFICE OF NATIONAL DRUG CONTROL POLICY 11 (2007).

[36] Hutto v. Davis, 454 U.S. 370, 374–75 (1982).

During the mid-80's, "baking soda base" appeared across the Caribbean, quickly spread into Miami, and was distributed across the United States. This form of cocaine freebase, easily manufactured from readily available materials, delivered an intense, inexpensive high.[37] During 1985, crack became a prominent issue of political and media attention, filling newspapers with stories of associated crime and the danger of crack. The 1980's political response was new "tough on crime" laws with longer sentences.[38]

The Anti-Drug Abuse Act of 1986 was the Federal government's response to the most recent drug menace, "crack," *Time* magazine's issue of the year. The new bill increased prison sentences for drug dealers and users, and significantly expanded asset forfeiture for drug crimes.[39] The emphasis on punishment and social control as a priority is made clear by the funding allocations: $1.7 billion was allocated for enforcement of the new act, in addition to the $2.2 billion previously allotted to anti-drug efforts; of the available funds, only 14% were for treatment,

---

[37] STEVEN R. BELENKO, CRACK AND THE EVOLUTION OF ANTI-DRUG POLICY 5 (1993).

[38] BELENKO, *supra* note 35, at 7.

[39] Anti-Drug Abuse Act of 1986, Pub. L.99-570, § 1152, 100 Stat. 3207, 3207-12 (1986).

education, or prevention efforts.[40] The 1988 Anti-Drug Act increased the already harsh punishments for drug offenses, requiring longer mandatory minimum sentences for crack related offenses.[41] The Anti-Drug Act also established the Office of National Drug Control Policy ("ONDCP") to set and oversee national drug control policy. [42]

By 1990, the number of people incarcerated in federal prisons for drug offenses had increased by over 500%.[43] Perceived harmfulness of the most commonly used drugs peaked at the very beginning of the 1990's likely due to the intense decade of intense drug law ernforcement throughout the United States and anti-drug education campaigns such as the famous "Just Say No" slogan and D.A.R.E. programs.[44] This perceived harmfulness decreased following the short peak, particularly for marijuana. The decrease in perceived harmfulness coincided with increasing rates of drug use among young adults, particularly college students.[45] The 1998

---

[40] BELENKO, *supra* note 35, at 14.
[41] Anti-Drug Abuse Act of 1988, 100 Pub. L. 690, § 6371,102 Stat. 4181, 4370 (1988).
[42] BELENKO, *supra* note 35, at 15.
[43] *Trends in Corrections Fact Sheet*, THE SENTENCING PROJECT, 3 http://sentencingproject.org/doc/publications/inc_Trends_in_Corrections_Fact_sh eet.pdf.
[44] L.D Johnston, P.M. O'Malley, J.G. Bachman, J.E. Schulenberg & R. A. Miech, *Monitoring the Future national survey results on drug use, 1975– 2015: Volume 2, College students and adults ages 19–55*, 260-290 (2016), http://monitoringthefuture.org/pubs/monographs/mtf-vol2_2015.pdf.
[45] *Id.*

Higher Education Act was passed to deter and remove drug use from college campuses by excluding students convicted of any drug crimes from receiving federal school loans.[46]

6.   2000 – 2015

A drug free America by 1995. This was the original mission of the ONDCP; each administration has modified both the goals and methods for measuring success. The ONDCP had five national goals in 2000, but by 2010 that was distilled to two goals: Curtail illicit drug consumption in America, and improve public health and safety of Americans by reducing consequences of Drug Abuse.[47] Internationally, the U.S. has increased cooperation with Mexico and Columbia in an attempt to curb the flow of drugs across the U.S.-Mexico border.[48] Efforts were also made to decrease opium exports from Afghanistan because the rise in international terrorism highlighted the link between middle eastern terrorism and the money-flushed opium trade.[49] Two prevalent

---

[46] Higher Education Amendments of 1998, 105 Pub. L. 244, § 120, 112 Stat. 1581, 1596–97 (1998).

[47] ROBINSON, *supra* note 33, at 37.

[48] OFFICE OF NATIONAL DRUG CONTROL POLICY, *The International Heroin Market*, https://www.whitehouse.gov/ondcp/global-heroin-market (last visited October 30, 2016).

[49] OFFICE OF NATIONAL DRUG CONTROL POLICY, *Afghanistan*, https://www.whitehouse.gov/ondcp/afghanistan-southwest-asia (last visited October 30, 2016).

trends in domestic drug policy since the beginning of the new millennium are sentencing adjustment and marijuana legalization.

In 2014, there were over 1.5 million people incarcerated in U.S. state and federal prisons, an increase of over 650% from 1974.[50] The Fair sentencing act of 2010 reduced the disparity between the sentences for powdered cocaine and crack cocaine and mitigated the impact of the draconian mandatory minimum sentencing for simple possession installed the 1980's.[51] Under the previous law, possession with intent to distribute 5 grams of crack cocaine, about the weight of a nickel, was punished as though equivalent to 500 grams of powdered cocaine, just over a pound. The Fair Sentencing act reduce that disparity to an 18-to-1 ratio between the two forms of cocaine.[52]

An increasing number of states are choosing to legalize marijuana for medical or recreational purposes, despite the continued federal prohibition. California was the first state to permit marijuana medicinally with the 1996 California Compassionate Use Act. In two landmark Supreme Court

---

[50] *Trends in Corrections Fact Sheet*, THE SENTENCING PROJECT, 3 http://sentencingproject.org/doc/publications/inc_Trends_in_Corrections_Fact_sheet.pdf.
[51] Fair Sentencing Act of 2010, 111 Pub. L. 220, 124 Stat. 2372 (2010).
[52] *Id.* ("striking "5 grams" and inserting "28 grams" for crack cocaine).

decisions, the federal prohibition of marijuana was upheld as a constitutional exercise of federal power and medical necessity is deemed not to be a valid exemption from federal prohibition.[53] Although there have been several medical studies showing the medical benefits and requests from the scientific community to study marijuana, the DEA refuses to re-schedule or de-schedule marijuana from its current position as a Schedule 1 controlled substance[54], same as heroin and a higher classification than methamphetamine. As of the November 8, 2016 election, there are 28 medical marijuana states, 9 recreational jurisdictions. This translates into a combined 50% of the U.S. population living in states that have legal marijuana access.

---

[53] *See* United States v. Oakland Cannabis Buyers' Coop., 532 U.S. 483 (2001); Gonzalez v. Raich, 545 U.S. 1 (2005).
[54] DEA.gov, "DEA announces actions related to marijuana and industrial hemp." (Aug. 11, 2016).

### III.	America's Current Crisis: Opiates

Everyone who has watched the news has likely encountered reports of rising drugs deaths, overdose, and addiction to heroin and prescription opiates. Pharmaceutical opiate drugs are made in laboratories, overly dispensed across the country, and often addict the prescribed user or the person who acquires the drugs. However, the origin, creation, and distribution of heroin is much less known than the effects it has on the end user.

Heroin is an opiate that produces a strong euphoric sensation in users, who commonly inject, smoke, or insufflate the narcotic. Heroin is very addictive. This drug originates primarily from Afghanistan and other Asian sources, but North American heroin is increasingly produced in Mexico or Columbia. Heroin manufacturing usually occurs in the origin country, and consists of deriving heroin as an opioid by product from opium poppies by a dangerous chemical process. The resulting heroin is more potent, more shippable, and more valuable than when its raw form.

Heroin use is on the rise nationally, seen by increasing arrests and overdose deaths and injuries. This is due to the increased use of prescription opioids and introduction of fentanyl to street opiates. Heroin production and possession is illegal across the United States; most states, Virginia included, apply felony charges and stiff fines to users who possess heroin. The following section will provide an overview of heroin, including its effects, production, use statistics, arrest statistics, and state-by-state punishment.

A. PHARMACOLOGY

Heroin is classified as an opioid drug; Heroin is specifically synthesized from morphine, a substance naturally produced by the opium poppy plant.[55] The drug was first discovered as diacetylmorphine in 1874 by C. R. Alder White, an English scientist who was performing experimentation on

---

[55] "Heroin" National Institute on Drug Abuse.
https://www.drugabuse.gov/publications/drugfacts/heroin

derivations of morphine. Near the end of the nineteenth century, Bayer, a German pharmaceutical company, marketed the new drug under the brand name "Heroin," derived from the German word "heroisch," meaning large powerful, or extreme. This was an apt description of the potential power of the newly discovered drug.[56] Heroin was initially described as an effective treatment of respiratory issues, ten times more effective than codeine, with significantly less toxicity.

Heroin is much more potent than morphine because of heroin's higher biological permeability than morphine. Once consumed, heroin passes into the blood brain barrier, and is converted to chemicals that quickly bind to the opioid receptors in the brain. The speed at which the heroin binds to the opioid receptors is responsible for the notable "rush" felt by heroin users. Opioids effect the body through the altered neurochemical activity; typical changes include a depression in breathing, release of chemicals in the limbic system that result in euphoric and pleasurable feelings, and acts as an analgesic, blocking pain signals sent through the nervous system.

---

[56] History of Heroin https://www.unodc.org/unodc/en/data-and-analysis/bulletin/bulletin_1953-01-01_2_page004.html#f001; http://methoide.fcm.arizona.edu/infocenter/index.cfm?stid=174

When Heroin is consumed by intravenous injection (injection directly into a vein) or smoking, users usually feel heroin's effects within seven to eight seconds. Intramuscular injection produces a more gradual onset of euphoric feelings, normally felt within five to eight minutes of injection. Insufflation is the slowest form of consumption, with peak effects felt after 10 to 15 minutes. Oral Administration is largely ineffective, and rarely employed as a heroin delivery method.[57]

When heroin is smoked or intravenously injected, users encounter two types of effects – the "rush" and the "high." First, a user may experience a rush immediately after administration, resulting from the rapid uptake of the heroin into the brain. This feeling is described as "an intense orgasmic feeling" that is felt throughout the body but localized strongly in the abdomen. The high follows the initial rush and can last between four and six hours. This sensation is described as a warm and pleasant feeling with general indifference to other stimulus around the user. During the high, users are often described as "going on the nod," which is exemplified by sitting or lying in a single location and alternating between falling asleep and waking up. Some users experience

---

[57] "Pharmacology"
http://methoide.fcm.arizona.edu/infocenter/index.cfm?stid=176

more of a stimulating effect, called "drive," which typically involves constant talking and activity from the user.[58]

B. DISTRIBUTION

Heroin, as a derivative of the opium by-product, starts in the parts of the world that grow and produce opium poppies. The major poppy producing countries have historically been in the "Golden Triangle" region of southeast Asia. However, production has increased among southwest Asia, particularly Afghanistan, which is responsible for nearly 80% of the world's opium.[59] Most of this opium proceeds through illegal smuggling channels into Europe. Although there was a steady decline in Afghan heroin production, Afghanistan produced 200,000 hectares of opium poppies, and 4100 metric tons of pure opium. In the 1990's, Latin America emerged as the primary producer of heroin for the United States and Canada, with the majority of production taking place in Mexico and Columbia. Mexico cultivates approximately

---

[58] National Institute on Drug Abuse, "Heroin" https://www.drugabuse.gov/publications/drugfacts/heroin

[59] Whitehouse.Gov, Office of National Drug Control Policy, "Global Heroin Market" https://www.whitehouse.gov/ondcp/global-heroin-market

28,000 hectares of opium poppy, with 70 potential metric tons of pure opium.[60]

Following production, smugglers can transport the heroin through various illegal market channels. Heroin from Afghanistan and other Asian destinations travel through intermediary stops such as UAE and Turkey before reaching their final European destinations, where the price and profitability for heroin is at its highest.

Much of the heroin used in the United States and Canada come from Latin American destinations. Distribution routes run through major metropolitan cities, with Northern cities as the target destination, where use and price is at its highest.

C. PRODUCTION

Illicit Heroin production generally occurs within the country where the opium is being produced. The processing of raw opium into morphine and heroin forms allows for easier transport due to the decreased weight and size. In Afghanistan, the opium growers transport raw product to clandestine heroin production

---

[60] Whitehouse.Gov, Office of National Drug Control Policy, "Mexico" https://www.whitehouse.gov/ondcp/mexico

labs, generally in the areas of the country that are remote and inaccessible by transportation.[61] In Mexico, processing heroin is performed by cartel chemists, often alongside the existing production of other laboratory produced drugs like methamphetamine. Heroin production in Mexico has increased significantly, over 59% from 2013 to 2014.[62] There is very little documentation regarding the illicit production of Heroin from any major sources; this process has been succesfully documented by United Nations personnel, specifically regarding the production of white Afghan heroin. [63]

The process starts with the selection of raw opium. The raw opium is selected based on its appearance, odor, and consistency. Once a quantity is selected, 70 kilograms in the observed case, the heroin production process begins.[64] The opium is then crushed and mixed into a solution of hot water and calcium oxide (anhydrous lime). Any additional packaging material would be separated from the opium in the solution and scooped off the

---

[61]Zerell, U. et al., Bulletin on Narcotics, vol. LVII, Nos. 1–2, p. 24 (2005)
http://www.unodc.org/pdf/research/Bulletin07/bulletin_on_narcotics_2007_Zerell.pdf
[62] 2016 International Narcotics Control Strategy Report
http://www.state.gov/j/inl/rls/nrcrpt/2016/vol1/253288.htm
[63] Zerell, U. et al., Bulletin on Narcotics, vol. LVII, Nos. 1–2, p. 12 (2005)
http://www.unodc.org/pdf/research/Bulletin07/bulletin_on_narcotics_2007_Zerell.pdf
[64] Id.

top of the solution. Following a 24-hour period, the entire solution would have become topped with a brown, oily liquid. This is a morphine solution, which is then syphoned off the raw opium solution. The raw components are then usually pressed to remove any additional morphine solution. The morphine solution is then precipitated using ammonium chloride. The precipitated morphine base was then filtered from the liquid solution using cloth filters. Approximately 7.8 kilograms of morphine base was produced.

Once the morphine base is extracted, the dried morphine is then mixed into another solution of acetic anhydride, which was given time to react and then heated. This produces a solution containing brown heroin base. The base is precipitated out of the solution by adding a sodium carbonate solution, filtered out, washed with hot water, and filtered again through a cloth. This brown heroin base is then dissolved into hydrochloric acid, and activated carbon is added to the mixture. This will result in a mostly clear solution.

Once the solution is mostly clear, the heroin base will be precipitated using diluted ammonia solution. The white heroin base is then filtered through a cloth. This white base is then dissolved into another solution of hydrochloric acid and acetone.

This mixture is again filtered, and then left to evaporate in a water bath. The remaining precipitate is a white, crystalline powder; this material is 74% pure white heroin. The final weight of this product is 3.9 kilograms.[65] This process describes high quality heroin being produced from minimal amounts of chemicals. This process varies between production country, and the type of heroin being produced.

D. DRUG ARREST STATISTICS: VIRGINIA CASE STUDY

Currently, heroin is a rising problem. Heroin use, and, even more alarming, overdoses are increasingly common, especially among young adults. The year 2013 was one of the deadliest years for heroin use since the turn of the century.[66] Cheap prices of heroin has prompted the migration of prescription drug users to the illicit narcotic with a single dose of heroin often costing only five dollars.[67] Because of the recent increases in overdose deaths, lawmakers have introduced multiple possible solution,

---

[65] *Id.* at 14-19.
[66] Johnson, Jenna and Rachel Weiner, "Overdose deaths from heroin galvanizing leaders in Maryland and Virginia." Washington Post, January 24, 2015 < https://www.washingtonpost.com/local/md-politics/overdose-deaths-from-heroin-galvanizing-leaders-in-maryland-and-virginia/2015/01/24/ef0c19fc-a305-11e4-9f89-561284a573f8_story.html >
[67] *Id.*

including wider availability of overdose treatments for first responders.

Crime statistics lend helpful insights into underlying drug use trends in the community. Take Virginia as an example. In Virginia, the rate of drug/narcotic arrests has increased steadily from 2009 to 2013, with a slight decrease in 2014. Drug/Narcotic violations are one of the leading causes of arrest in the Commonwealth.[68] In 2014, there were 37,924 reported drug/narcotic arrests; this number includes drug equipment violations. March was the most active month with 3,663 reported arrests, and December had the lowest number of drug arrests at 2,529.[69] Virginia Beach had the most reported narcotic offenses of any jurisdiction, with 3,319 drug arrests by city and state police. Chesapeake took the number two spot, topping Richmond and neighboring Hampton Roads cities, with 2,520 total drug arrests in 2014. Drug offenses are the second leading cause of arrest in Chesapeake, behind only simple assault.[70]

---

[68] Department of State Police, 2014 Crime in Virginia, p. 4 (2015) (drug/narcotics violations and related drug equipment crimes make up 28.4% of people arrested for Group A offenses).
[69] *Id.* at 65.
[70] *Id.* at 96–99.

Marijuana arrests were the most prevalent, constituting approximately 61% of the total drug arrests. Heroin accounted for 1,912 arrests, which is only 5% of the total drug arrests in Virginia in 2014. Combing all the opiate drugs such as morphine and opium, opiate drug arrests accounted for 5.6% of total drug arrests at 2,092 arrests.[71] This does not include any numbers of arrests from "other narcotic," "Other Drugs," or "Unknown Drug Type," which total 7,506 arrests, and may include types of opiates not specifically identified in the arrest.[72] Fortunately, there were only five reported heroin arrests for people under the age of 17, and only ten combined opiate arrests of minors. Although this is not directly correlative to opiate use among minors, it at least is circumstantial evidence of lower use among minors. Among adults, the largest number of heroin arrests occur among 25-29-year olds. This age group accounts for the largest number of arrests for nearly all drugs.[73] Combined with the second largest arrested age group, 30-34-year-olds, people aged 25-34 account for nearly 44% of the 2014 heroin arrests in Virginia.

---

[71] *See Id.* at 66.

[72] *Id.* ("other narcotic" accounted for 1,821 arrests, "Other Drugs" accounted for 948 arrests, and "Unknown Drug Type" accounted for 4,737 arrests).

[73] *Id.* (PCP arrests among 30-34 year-old age group is the single area 25-29 year old do not have the highest use).

E.   HEROIN USE STATISTICS

First, it is important to view the national trends regarding heroin use as it provides context for the use within a state or city. Between 2000 and 2013, the drug poisoning death related to heroin quadrupled, with most of that increase occurring since 2010.[74] Men are much more likely to both use and overdose on heroin, with 6,525 deaths among men and 1,732 deaths among women. The general demographic of the average heroin user has shifted dramatically in the past two decades. The primary user of heroin in 2000 was black men aged 45-64; in 2013, the primary demographic using heroin were non-Hispanic white males age 18-44, and at over three times the rate of black men in 2000.[75] In addition to the highest rate of use, males between 25-44 had the highest rate of heroin overdoses. This is reflective of the high rate of arrest for heroin among this age group. Although the overall numbers and rate of heroin use and overdose has significantly increased since 2000, deaths related to other opioid analgesics are

---

[74]Hedegaard, Holly; Li-Hui Chen, and Margaret Warner, *Drug-poisoning Deaths Involving Heroin: United States, 2000–2013*, NCHS Data Brief No. 190 (2015) <http://www.cdc.gov/nchs/data/databriefs/db190.htm>.
[75] *Id.*

remain significantly higher in number and the rate of these deaths has not increased significantly since 2006.[76]

Returning to Virginia, heroin use and drug-induced deaths are both lower than the national average.[77] Virginia and the national average both place opioid hospitalizations and deaths higher than heroin specifically.[78] Like the national increase in heroin use, there has been a significant increase in heroin use and fatal overdoses since 2010, with an increase of 44% between 2014 and 2015 alone. Although the number of prescription opioids has remained nominally the same over the same time, this finding is somewhat deceptive when the introduction of illicit fentanyl is taken into consideration.

Fentanyl is labeled as a prescription opioid because it is mass produced by American pharmaceutical companies, but there has been a significant increase in illicit fentanyl production from Asia and South America. Overall death from non-fentanyl prescriptions opioids has decreased, but the deaths associated with

---

[76] *Id.*

[77]Executive Office of the President, *Virginia Drug Control Update* (2011) <https://www.whitehouse.gov/sites/default/files/docs/state_profile_-_virginia.pdf>.

[78]Health and Criminal Justice Data Committee, *Report to the Governor's Task Force on Prescription Drug and Heroin Abuse*, (2016) <http://www.dhp.virginia.gov/taskforce/minutes/20160504/HealthCriminalJustice DataCteRpt05042016.pdf>.

fentanyl has increased over 60% in the last year. Additionally, the form of delivery has changed, from the pharmaceutical standard transdermal patch to the now common powder or residue forms of fentanyl. This drug is often combined with heroin or used in conjunction with heroin. This relatively new combination is rapidly becoming the common cause of opioid related deaths, with an increase of 267% percent between 2013–14, and another 332% increase between 2014–15.[79]

F.   50-STATE SURVEY OF HEROIN POSSESSION STATUTES

The current approach to heroin use across the states has been a trend towards punitive prohibition. "Punitive Prohibition" refers to drug policies that focus on penal sanctions, particularly incarceration, for users of illegal drugs.[80] This approach is occasionally referred to as the "criminal justice" or "moral" model, presuming that "illicit drug use is morally wrong" and should be thus criminalized.[81] This model has been exemplified in U.S. federal and state-level domestic drug policy, and has become the

---

[79] *Id.*

[80] Aoyagi, Melissa T., *Note: Beyond Punitive Prohibition: Liberalizing The Dialogue On International Drug Policy*, 37 N.Y.U. J. Int'l L. & Pol. 555, 560

[81] *Id.*

international standard with the passage of several international

drug polices influenced heavily by the United States.[82]

i. FELONY THRESHOLD

The policy of punitive prohibition is clearly present in the

drug laws across the states. Thirty-nine (39) out of the fifty states

currently apply a varying level of felony charge to any possession

of heroin, even on the first offense.[83] The states that do not require

a felony charge have three alternatives imposing felony heroin

possession: repeated offenders, elevated amount, or no felony

possession.

The repeat offender states impose a felony charge on

heroin possessors who have multiple possession offenses.[84] The

elevated amount states put minimum limits on felony possession

charges.[85] The amount required to trigger a felony possession

---

[82] *Id.* at 577–81 (identifying the international drug treaty structure, consisting of Single Convention on Narcotic Drugs of 1961 as amended by the 1972 Protocol, the 1971 Convention on Psychotropic Substances, and the Convention Against Illicit Traffic in Narcotic Drugs and Psychotropic Substances of 1988).

[83] These State's statues do not impose a felony on first-time any amount heroin possession: Pennsylvania, Iowa, Tennessee, Rhode Island, Washington D.C., Maryland, Massachusetts, Wyoming, New York, Mississippi, West Virginia, and South Carolina.

[84] Pennsylvania, Maryland, and Massachusetts charges heroin possession as a felony on the second offense. 35 Pa. Stat. §§ 780-113(a)(16), (b); Md. Crim. Law Code Ann. § 5-601; Mass. Gen. Laws Ann. ch. 94C, § 34. Iowa charges heroin possession as a felony on the third offense. Iowa Code § 124.401(5).

[85] These states are New York, Mississippi, Delaware, 16 Del. Code § 4756, and South Carolina, S.C. Code Ann. § 44-53-370(d)(4).

varies; for example, New York requires greater than one-eighth (1/8) ounce of heroin, whereas Mississippi only requires greater than two dosage units, a drastically smaller quantity of heroin.[86] Some states simply do not apply felony charges to heroin possession for small amounts, but may have increased penalties for repeated offenders.[87]

ii. POSSESSION PENALTIES

Possession penalties vary widely across the United States. As stated previously, most states' statutes authorize a felony charge for any heroin possession, regardless of how small the amount. Even within this category, however, there is significant variance between the applicable penalties. For example, Kansas and Kentucky, although both felony possession states, allow parole rather than incarceration for first time offenders.[88]

There is also a significant range between possible penalties across the states. In states not allowing parole for first offenders, possible incarceration of heroin possessors ranges from six months in local jail in Washington D.C. or West Virginia, to over ten

---

[86] *Compare* N.Y. Penal Law § 220.09(1) (McKinney) *with* Miss. Code. Ann. § 41-29-139(c).

[87] Tennessee, Washington D.C., Wyoming, and West Virginia apply misdemeanor charges to heroin possession. Tenn. Code. Ann. § 39-17-418(a); D.C. Code § 48-904.01(d)(1); Wyo. Stat. Ann. § 35-7-1031(c)(i); W. Va. Code § 60A-4-401(c).

[88] Kan. Stat. Ann. § 21-5706(a); Ky. Rev. Stat. § 218A.1415.

years' incarceration in Virginia and seven other states.[89] Virginia does give the sentencing party, whether that be a jury or a judge, the discretion to only sentence the convicted person to 12 months in jail rather than a prison term.[90] Georgia and South Carolina even authorize up to fifteen years in prison for simple heroin possession.[91] The average term of available incarceration is 5.34 years, and the median term of incarceration is five years.

In addition to the long terms of incarceration legally required or permitted, all state laws call for or allow the imposition of fines and civil penalties. Much like the incarceration permitted under each state's law, the fines and penalties imposed vary wildly.[92] States that treat heroin possession different criminally may apply the same financial penalty. Look at California and West Virginia, which classify heroin possession as a felony and misdemeanor,

---

[89] *Compare* D.C. Code § 48-904.01(d)(1) (heroin possession is a misdemeanor that can receive up to six months in jail); W. Va. Code § 60A-4-401(c) (heroin possession is a misdemeanor that can receive between 90 to 180 in jail) *with* Va. Code § 18.2-250(a) (heroin possession is a felon with maximum allowed incarnation of 10 years); Utah Code Ann. § 58-37-8(2) (heroin possession is a felon with maximum allowed incarnation of 10 years). Louisiana, Oklahoma, Oregon, and South Dakota also allow up to ten (10) years of incarceration for heroin possession.

[90] Va. Code Ann. § 18.2-10.

[91] Ga. Code § 16-13-30(c); S.C. Code Ann. § 44-53-370(d)(4).

[92] Court costs and any other fees associated with a criminal trial and conviction, e.g., attorney's fees or treatment costs, are not included in these discussion. These costs can, in summation, be substantial.

respectively. However, both states apply a $1,000 fine for heroin possession, two of the lowest allowable fines.[93]

Statutory maximums for fines range from $1,000 to $250,000.[94] Most states' fines permitted under law fall under $25,000, but there are currently 16 states that permit fines of $25,000 or more. Even Washington D.C., which classifies heroin possession as a misdemeanor, allows for the possibility of a large fine of $75,000.[95] Virginia allows for a fine up to $2,500.[96] Because of the large variance in the allowable fines, the average permitted fine is quite hefty at $21,629; the median permitted fine is $10,000.

---

[93] *See* Cal. Health & Safety Code § 11350(a) (allowing fine up to $1000); W. Va. Code § 60A-4-401(c) (allowing fine up to $1000).
[94] Oregon allows up to $250,000 fine for heroin possession, a class B felony. *See* Or. Rev. Stat. §§ 475.854, 161.625.
[95] D.C. Code § 48-904.01(d)(1).
[96] Va. Code § 18.2-250(a).

IV.   **Collateral Consequences of Drug Offenses**

This section analyzes the collateral consequences of drug offenses, including topics such as education, employment, and basic American rights. However, it will not examine the reasonableness, proportionality, or effect of the primary punishment. State and federal law impose substantial criminal penalties for possession, sale, or manufacture of any drug. The punishment imposed by some states for simple drug possession are equivalent to crimes such as sexual battery,[97] or punished more severely than maiming while driving intoxicated or strangulation.[98]

Collateral consequences are additional statutory sanctions and penalties applied in addition to the criminal fines and penalties imposed by a judge or jury at sentencing. Some collateral consequences are common to all felony convictions, such as the loss of voting rights. However, even misdemeanor drug offenses

---

[97] *Compare* LA. STAT. ANN § 14:43.1 (2016) (sexual battery can be imprisoned up to 10 years, with or without hard labor, without parole or suspension of sentence) *with* §40:966 (2016) (possession of a narcotic Schedule 1 drug shall be punished with imprisonment at hard labor for not less than four years nor more than 10 years).

[98] *Compare* VA. CODE ANN. §§ 18.2-51.4, 51.6 (2016) (Maiming, etc., of another resulting from driving while intoxicated and Strangulation of Another both class 6 felonies) *with* § 18.2-250 (2016) (possession of schedule I or II controlled substance is class 5 felony).

face specially-targeted statutory consequences that are often unannounced at sentencing. In addition to the collateral consequences highlighted, social consequences often result from a drug conviction, whether that be loss of social standing or stigmatization among the local community, or even within the person's family.

Imposition of collateral consequences are based in federal, state, or a mixture of state and federal laws and regulations. Federal and state laws automatically impose additional penalties for conviction of drug offenses. Some consequences imposed by federal law permit states to opt-out or extend rights and privileges to citizens convicted of drug crimes. However, even residents of American states more progressive towards drug policy still face significant collateral effects of even minor drug offenses.

Six major collateral consequences create substantial barriers to successful reintegration of citizens back into their communities: voting rights restrictions, education funding restrictions, housing assistance restrictions, welfare ineligibility, employment exclusion, and driver's license suspension.

1.   <u>Voting</u>

Voting is a fundamental liberty in America constitutionally afforded to all races[99], sexes[100], and young adults.[101] In the majority of states, citizens convicted of a felony face voting disenfranchisement, the last surviving "major restriction of the voting right of adult citizens" in the United States.[102] Felony disenfranchisement is an issue that rose to recent national prominence after the Virginia Supreme Court blocked Gov. McAuliffe's move to restore voting rights *en mass* to thousands of Virginians with felony records.[103] There are two levels of this constitutional right: federal interpretation, and a variety of state approaches.

Exclusion of convicted felons from elections is explicitly allowed by the constitution. The Fourteenth Amendment extended voting rights to men in the age of majority regardless of race, color, or former status of servitude.[104] This amendment does make an exception: voting may be "abridged" for "participation in

---

[99] U.S. CONST. amend XV.
[100] U.S. CONST. amend. XIX.
[101] U.S. CONST. amend. XXVI.
[102] Alec Ewald, *"Civil Death": The Ideological Paradox of Criminal Disenfranchisement Law in the United States*, 2002 WIS. L. REV. 1045, 1045 (2002).
[103] Howell v. McAuliffe, 788 S.E.2d 706 (Va. 2016).
[104] U.S. CONST. amend. XIX.

rebellion, or other crime." Voting restriction based on a felony conviction was tested in the U.S. Supreme Court case *Richard v. Ramirez*. In that case, a citizen convicted of a felony was disenfranchised under state law, and challenged that status under the equal protection clause. The Supreme Court held that felony voting restriction were permissible under the text of Fourteenth Amendment and consistent with the historical and judicial history of application of the rule.[105] Federal courts have since interpreted "broad felon disenfranchisement provisions [as] presumptively constitutional." [106] Federal voting rights are dependent upon the state law where that person resides.[107]

Voting for representation is an important and fundamental right that sparked the American Revolution against Great Britain; barring this basic civic participation further degrades the dignity and civic involvement of returning citizens.[108] The recent release of a record number of offenders incarcerated under the harsh anti-drug laws of the 1980's[109] has resulted in a

---

[105] Richardson v. Ramirez, 418 U.S. 24, 54–55 (1974).
[106] Anbessa v. McDonnell, Civil Action No. 3:13CV138-HEH, 2015 U.S. Dist. LEXIS 48133, 4-5 (E.D. Va. Apr. 13, 2015) (quoting Simmons v. Galvin, 575 F.3d 24, 32 (1st Cir. 2009))
[107] *Id.* at 1057.
[108] Pinard, *supra* note 64, at 471.
[109] Michael Pinard, *Collateral Consequences of Criminal Convictions: Confronting issues of Race and Dignity*, 85 N.Y.U. L. Rev. 457, 461 (2010).

large swell of disqualified voters who are no longer incarcerated, but are either on parole, probation, or have served their entire sentence.[110]

Each states' disenfranchisement and restoration procedures vary greatly, ranging from immediate and indefinite disenfranchisement following conviction to disenfranchisement only when incarcerated.[111] Virginia's permanent disenfranchisement policy is in the Commonwealth's Constitution, allowing for restoration only by governor mandate.[112] Maine and Vermont take a different approach: convicted felons do not lose the right to vote even during incarceration.[113] Broad, permanent disenfranchisement of former felons when the crime is unrelated to election or government fraud creates a collateral consequence that can last far beyond the end of criminal punishment for minor felonies.

---

[110] Ewald, *supra* note 57, at 1055.
[111] Ewald, *supra* note 57, at 1054.
[112] VA. CONST. art. II, § 1 ("No person who has been convicted of a felony shall be qualified to vote unless his civil rights have been restored by the Governor or other appropriate authority.").
[113] Ewald, *supra* note 57, at 1054 n.23 (Vermont will remove voting rights only for persons convicted of election-related felonies.).

2.	<u>Education</u>

The current policy of mandatory college funding exclusion for even minor drug offenses was a result of Congress' best intentions. Campus crime was a topic of discussion before both houses of Congress in the late 1990's; conversations focused on rising drug crime rates on college campuses.[114] As a result, Congress added a provision to the 1998 Higher Education Act (HEA) amendments aimed at reducing drug crimes on college campuses. HEA passed with bipartisan support and near unanimity.[115]

The current HEA provision controlling student eligibility for federal grants or loans prohibits any person convicted of any state or federal drug crime, whether misdemeanor or felony[116]. The eligibility restriction was bifurcated for sale and possession convictions. Convictions for sale of controlled substances triggers a two-year ineligibility, and a subsequent sale conviction results in

---

[114] Domestic Social Policy Division, CRS, *Student Eligibility: Drug Convictions and Federal Aid*, CRS-2004-DSP-0096, 2 (2004).

[115] *Id.*; UNITED STATES CONGRESS, *H.R. 6, 105th Congress (1997 – 1998) Roll Call Vote* (https://www.congress.gov/bill/105th-congress/house-bill/6/all-actions?overview=closed&q=%7B%22roll-call-vote%22%3A%22all%22%7D) (House – 414 yea, 4 nay; Senate – 96 yea, 1 no) (last visited October 30, 2016.).

[116] 20 U.S.C § 1091(r) (2016) ("A student who is convicted of any offense under any Federal or State law involving the possession or sale of a controlled substance for conduct that occurred during a period of enrollment for which the student was receiving any grant, loan, or work assistance under this title shall not be eligible to receive any grant, loan, or work assistance under this title from the date of that conviction for the [time period].").

indefinite ineligibility. A student convicted of a first-time possession charge is ineligible for one year; two years after a second charge. A person convicted of three possession charges is indefinitely ineligible. [117] The federal application for student aid, sometimes called the FAFSA, has questioned applicants about history of drug convictions since 2001. Over 250,000 applicants were excluded through self-reporting or failure to report in just the first three school years.[118]

Once convicted, eligibility for student loans can be restored three ways: passage of time, successful drug rehabilitation treatment, or conviction is "rendered nugatory."[119] If the ineligibility is one or two years, the convicted person can wait until their restriction period expires and he or she becomes eligible again. However, for those rendered indefinitely ineligible, a drug rehabilitation treatment program must be completed, which can be cost-prohibitive without any or sufficient insurance coverage.[120]

---

[117] *Id.*

[118] GAO-05-238, *Denial of Federal Benefits*, 52-56 (Sept. 2005) (totaling 263,534 applicants excluded: 2001-02 - 58,929 self-reported, 48,642 no answer; 2002-03 – 42,537 self-reported, 37,451 no answer; 2003-04 – 41,061 self-reported, 34,914 no answer).

[119] 20 U.S.C. § 1091(r)(2) (2016).

[120] *See* Leah Miller, *How Much Does Addiction Rehab Cost?* Rehabs.Com. http://www.rehabs.com/about/how-much-does-rehab-cost/ (Standard inpatient addiction treatment can cost between $2,000 and $25,000 and outpatient programs can cost up to $10,000 for 30-programs.)

These programs must comply with certain basic criteria, such as professional licensing and perform at least two unannounced drug tests. The completion and passage of the program and the random testing will allow the convicted person to become eligible again for student loans.[121] The only other way to restore eligibility is to have the drug conviction "rendered nugatory," meaning it must be reversed, set aside, or expunged, often requiring additional costs for attorney fees or court costs.[122]

College students without significant financial assets who are charged even with misdemeanor possession are effectively prevented from attending school for the period during which federal funding is withheld.[123] Students seeking financial aid are more likely to be low-income and in an ethnic minority, and access to federal assistance has increased the number of minority students in higher education.[124] Comparing that with high drug conviction rates for young members of racial minorities, this exclusion has

---

[121] 34 CFR 668.40.

[122] *Id.*

[123] 20 U.S.C 1091(r)(1) (2016); Robin Levi & Judith Appel, *Collateral Consequences: Denial of Basic Social Services Based Upon Drug Use*, DRUG POLICY ALLIANCE, 3–4 (2003), http://www.drugpolicy.org/docUploads/Postincarceration_abuses_memo.pdf.

[124] Christopher M. Brown et al., *Walking a Policy Tightrope: Balancing Educational Opportunity and Criminal Justice in Federal Student Financial Aid*, 71 THE JOURNAL OF NEGRO EDUCATION no. 3, 2002, at 233, 234.

disproportionally affected groups who benefit the most from federal student aid.[125]

Monitoring The Future's annual survey on drug use among college-age adults shows drug use and exposure was increasing prior to the passage of the HEA, with an increase of 29% regular drug use prevalence in 1991 to 38% in 1998.[126] Use and availability of illegal drugs continued to grow despite the implementation of the HEA, with 41% of college-age adults using illegal drugs in 2015, driven mainly by marijuana use; in 2015 over 90% of college age adults say that marijuana could be acquired "fairly" or "very easy."[127] The HEA's heavy cost of minority exclusion has reduced opportunity for the students who need federal loans the most but failed to cure college campuses of the dangerous drug culture.

3.		Housing

Per a minimalist theory of human rights, shelter is a basic need for all people. In the United States, a heated, enclosed, semiprivate dwelling is a societal need and considered a minimum

---

125 *Id.* at 234–35.
126 Johnston, *supra* note 42, at 376.
127 *Id.*

living standard.[128] A combined 4 million low-income families are served through the federal government's three primary housing programs: The Public Housing program, the Housing Choice Voucher Program, and Section 8 project-based rental assistance.[129] Even federal housing assistance for such a basic need as housing is jeopardized for citizens and their families who have been charged with drug crimes.

Under the guidance of the U.S. Department of Housing and Urban Development ("HUD"), each state's Public Housing Authority ("PHA") has wide discretion in the application of many regulations.[130] Federal legislation has continually added to the power and discretion of local PHA over the admission of drug offenders to federally-funded housing programs. PHAs have discretion over exclusion of applicants with any criminal histories that may indicate possible risks to community safety.[131] In 1990, the federal government mandated PHA's ban re-admission of

---

[128] John Pearson, *Is Miller's Minimalist Approach to Human Rights Obligations Coherent?* 58 THEORIA: A JOURNAL OF SOCIAL AND POLITICAL THEORY, no. 129, 2011, at 35, 38–39.

[129] A. Marah, et al., *Alcohol, Drug, and Criminal History Restrictions in Public Housing,* Cityscape: A Journal of Policy Development and Research, U.S. DEPARTMENT OF HOUSING AND URBAN DEVELOPMENT, OFFICE OF POLICY DEVELOPMENT AND RESEARCH, Vol. 15, no. 3, 2013, Pp. 38.

[130] Pinard, *supra* note 64, at 490.

[131] The Quality Housing and Work Responsibility Act of 1998, Pub. L. 105-276, 112 Stat. 2461 (1998).

tenants evicted for criminal drug activity for at least three years.[132] PHAs discretion is bound by a federal regulation structure requiring denial of certain applicants, such those with a pattern of abusing drugs and alcohol.[133]

In addition to denial of admission to public housing programs, "One Strike" housing laws require eviction for "any drug-related criminal activity on or off such premises, engaged in by a public housing tenant, any member of the tenant's household, or any guest or other person under the tenant's control."[134] PHA leases required clauses allowing eviction of any tenant engaged in drug use or any behaviors that could threaten the safety of other tenants.[135] The tenant's knowledge of drug activity by other occupants, guests, or invitees is presumed, only overcome by a preponderance of the evidence.[136]

The Supreme Court has affirmed such evictions, holding tenants responsible for the actions of household members or guests, even if the criminal drug use was unknown to the leasing

---

[132] Cranston-Gonzalez National Affordable Housing Act of 1990, Pub. L. 101–625, 104 Stat 4079 (1990).
[133] 24 CFR § 982.553 (2017).
[134] 42 U.S.C. 1437(d) (2012).
[135] Anti-Drug Abuse Act of 1988, 100 Pub. L. 690,102 Stat. 4181 (1988).
[136] *Id.*

tenant and occurred outside the home.[137] For example, Virginia allows termination of tenancy without waiting for a drug conviction; the landlord must prove the illegal drug use of the "tenant, the tenant's authorized occupants, or the tenant's guests or invitees" by a mere "preponderance of the evidence." [138] These policies are strong incentives to not allow current or recovering drug-using relatives to cohabitate since any relapse or even history of drug-related activity poses a threat to the tenant's lease, potentially resulting in homelessness of the offender.[139]

4.   <u>Welfare Assistance Programs</u>

Low-income Citizens convicted of federal or state drug felonies face restrictions to welfare assistance, including Temporary Assistance to Needy Families (TANF) and SNAP, formerly Food Stamp, programs.[140] The Personal Responsibility and Work Opportunity Reconciliation Act of 1996 excluded felony drug offenders from receiving federal or state benefits

---

[137] *See* U.S. Department of Housing and Urban Development v. Rucker, 535 U.S. 125, 136 (2002) ("Sec. 1437(d) requires lease terms that give local public housing authorities the discretion to terminate the lease of a tenant when a member of the household or a guest engages in drug-related activity, regardless of whether the tenant knew, or should have known, of the drug-related activity.").

[138] VIRGINIA DEPARTMENT OF HOUSING AND COMMUNITY DEVELOPMENT, *Landlord-Tenant Handbook*, 35 (2016), http://www.dhcd.virginia.gov/images/Housing/Landload-Tenant-Handbook.pdf; VA. CODE ANN. §55-248.31 (2016),

[139] Levi, *supra* note 75, at 2.

[140] 21 U.S.C. 862(a) (2012); Levi, *supra* note 74, at 4–5.

indefinitely[141], but allowed states three options for enforcement: unaltered adoption of the federal law, a state law defining a limited period of benefit prohibition, or a state law to completely opt out of the prohibition.[142] Twelve states have adopted the federal lifetime ban on TANF, but only ten apply the ban to SNAP benefits.[143] Virginia permanently bans both, but allows an exemption for citizens convicted only of felony possession.[144]

On the other hand, eleven states and the District of Columbia have opted out of disqualifying drug felons for TANF, and twenty-two states and D.C. have opted out of SNAP disqualifications.[145] The remaining states have modified the federal ban, twenty-seven for TANF and eighteen for SNAP,

---

[141] Child Care and Development Block Grant Amendments of 1996, Pub. L 104-193, 110 Stat. 2105 (1996); 21 U.S.C. 862a (2012).
[142] 7 C.F.R. § 273.11(m).
[143] Maggie McCarty et al. "Drug Testing and Crime-Related Restrictions in TANF, SNAP, and Housing Assistance" CONGRESSIONAL RESEARCH SERVICE 9, 12 (2015) (TANF – Alaska, Arizona, Delaware, Georgia, Mississippi, Missouri, Nebraska, South Carolina, South Dakota, Texas, Virginia, West Virginia; SNAP – Alaska, Arizona, Florida, Georgia, Indiana, Mississippi, Nebraska, South Carolina, Virginia, West Virginia).

[144] Va. Code Ann. § 63.2-505.2 (2012).
[145] McCarty, *supra* note 101, at 12 (TANF – Alabama, District of Columbia, New Hampshire, New Mexico, New York, Ohio, Oklahoma, Oregon, Rhode Island, Vermont, Washington, Wyoming; SNAP - SNAP – Alabama, California, Delaware, District of Columbia, Illinois, Iowa, Maine, Massachusetts, New Hampshire, New Jersey, New Mexico, New York, Ohio, Oklahoma, Oregon, Pennsylvania, Rhode Island, South Dakota, Utah, Vermont, Texas, Washington, Wyoming).

generally requiring a drug test for admission or continued enrollment in the benefit programs.[146]

The wild variance among the states is a major impediment to low-income reentering citizens' ability to travel freely between the states, a long-recognized constitutional right.[147] For example, Maryland has a modified welfare ban for recipients with drug felonies that requires the recipient's passing a drug screen.[148] Just south is Washington D.C., which does not disqualify recipients with drug felonies from SNAP or TANF. A bit further south is Virginia, which adopted the federal drug felony ban on TANF and SNAP benefits. Maryland and D.C. are comparably accessible for a non-drug-using citizen with a drug felony, but Virginia is inaccessible for many drug offenders who do qualify for the

---

[146] *Id.* (TANF - Arkansas, California, Colorado, Connecticut, Florida, Hawaii, Idaho, Illinois, Indiana, Iowa, Kansas, Kentucky, Louisiana, Maine, Maryland, Massachusetts, Michigan, Minnesota, Montana, Nevada, New Jersey, North Carolina, North Dakota, Pennsylvania Tennessee, Utah, Wisconsin; SNAP – Arkansas, Colorado, Connecticut, Hawaii, Idaho, Kansas, Kentucky, Louisiana, Maryland, Michigan, Minnesota, Missouri, Montana, Nevada, North Carolina, North Dakota, Tennessee, Wisconsin).

[147] Shapiro v. Thompson, 394 U.S. 618, 631 (1969) ("Thus, the purpose of deterring the in-migration of indigents cannot serve as justification for the classification created by the one-year waiting period, since that purpose is constitutionally impermissible.").

[148] MD. HUM. SERVS. CODE ANN. §5-601 (2016); MD. CODE REGS. 07.03.03.09 (2016).

statutory exception if the person relies on welfare assistance for personal or family sustenance.[149]

5. Employment

Economic self-reliance following a drug conviction is seriously impaired by a felony conviction. Currently, there are numerous federal and state restrictions on hiring applicants with criminal records for a variety of positions in private and public sectors.[150] The Equal Employment Opportunity Commission ("EEOC") has interpreted Title VII of the Civil Rights Act of 1964 to restrict employment discrimination based solely upon a criminal history, and a valid "business necessity" is required for a refusal to hire.[151] The EEOC recognizes that discrimination based on criminal history has an adverse impact on Black and Hispanic applicants considering the elevated conviction rates of those populations.[152]

---

[149] *See* 2012 Va. AG LEXIS 5 (2012) (clarifying that Va. Code § 63.2-505.2 only applies to citizens convicted of possession offenses under Va. Code § 18.2-250).

[150] Pinard, *supra* note 64, at 492.

[151] EQUAL EMPLOYMENT OPPORTUNITY COMMISSION, *EEOC Policy Statement on the Issue of Conviction Records under Title VII of the Civil Rights Act of 1964, as amended, 42 U.S.C. § 2000e et seq.* (1982) https://www.eeoc.gov/policy/docs/convict1.html.

[152] *Id. See also* Green v. Mo. P. R. Co., 523 F.2d 1290, 1297 (8th Cir. 1975) ([A] sweeping disqualification for employment resting solely on past behavior can violate Title VII where that employment practice has a disproportionate racial impact and rests upon a tenuous or insubstantial basis.").

Despite federal statutory protections, enforcement of protective laws are often weak. Only a few states having comprehensive laws governing consideration of criminal conviction during hiring.[153] Virginia employers are only restricted from requesting expunged criminal records.[154] Alternatively, Hawai'i requires most public or private employers to request criminal background information only after a conditional offer of employment has been extended to the applicant, and can only consider convictions occurring in the last ten years.[155]

6.   Driver's License Suspension

Reliable transportation is often a requirement to maintain gainful employment; suspension of a driver's license for drug crimes can be a crippling by restricting an offender's ability to drive himself or family members to various obligations. For example, the Virginia Beach-Norfolk-Newport News Metropolitan Statistical Area, representing Hampton Roads, is the 37th most populous region in the United States, has a population exceeding 1.7 million residents[156] spread over 526 square miles.

---

[153] Pinard, *supra* note 64, at 493–94.

[154] VA. CODE ANN § 19.2-392.4 (2016).

[155] HAW. REV. STAT. §§ 378-2.5(b)-(d) (2016).

[156] U.S. CENSUS BUREAU, POPULATION DIVISION, *Annual Estimates of the Resident Population: April 1, 2010 to July 1, 2015,* (March 2016) http://factfinder.census.gov/faces/tableservices/jsf/pages/productview.xhtml?src=bkmk.

Most Hampton Roads commuters averaged 20 miles per day with average travel times between 26 and 31 minutes' travel to destinations outside of their resident city.[157] Many employees' jobs are explicitly dependent on having reliable transportation. In such an environment, a driver's license becomes increasingly important for travel to employment or education.

The large impact of losing a driver's license in communities that require reliable personal transportation due to lacking public transit systems makes this collateral consequence more than a personal inconvenience. Seventeen States cumulatively housing 48% of the nation's population require mandatory suspension of driver's licenses for misdemeanor and felony drug offenses, even if the offense did not occur while driving.[158]

---

[157] *HOV Attitudinal Research among Hampton Roads Commuters.* VIRGINIA DEPARTMENT OF TRANSPORTATION, (July 2002), http://www.virginiadot.org/info/researchdatabase/uploads/02003/final%20report-hov%20attitudinal%20research%20among%20hampton%20roads%20commuters.htm (last visited November 1, 2016).

[158] Reefer sanity: States abandon driver's license suspensions for drug offenses, The Clemency Report, July 15, 2015, http://clemencyreport.org/drivers-license-suspensions-drug-offenses-state-state-list/ . ("Virginia, 29,086; New York, 28,679; Florida, 24,430; Texas, 23,821; Pennsylvania, 19,969; Arkansas, 4,610; Iowa, 4,056; The other suspending jurisdictions: Alabama, Delaware, Georgia, Indiana, Massachusetts, Mississippi, Oklahoma, Ohio, New Jersey Wisconsin, plus Washington, D.C. and Puerto Rico.").

The Commonwealth of Virginia had the largest number of suspensions for drug convictions at 29,086 in 2010.[159] Until recently, Virginia Code automatically suspends the driver's license of any person convicted of a drug crime or deferred under a first-time drug offense program for a period of six months.[160] Courts have discretion only to allow a restricted license for the express purpose of work, school, childcare, and religious worship[161]; any deviation from those destinations will result in additional charges for driving on a restricted license.[162] Through the reform efforts of cannabis reform organizations such as Virginia NORML, Virginia's law now has given some discretion to judges in possession cases not involving a vehicle.[163] Other states give judges more discretion over licensure suspension, such as Wisconsin, which gives courts discretion in suspending driving privileges, and the range of time, from 6 months to 5 years.[164]

---

[159] *Id.*; *Best Practices Guide to Reducing Suspended Drivers*, American Association of Motor Vehicle Administrators (Feb. 2013), http://www.aamva.org/Suspended-and-Revoked-Drivers-Working-Group/.
[160] VA. CODE ANN. § 18.2-259.1(A) (2016).
[161] VA. CODE ANN. § 18.2-259.1(C) (2016).
[162] VA. CODE ANN. § 46.2-301 (2016).
[163] Virginia Senate Bill 784 (2017).
[164] WIS. STAT. § 961.50 (2016).

7.   Racial Disparity in Enforcement

Since their inception, drug laws have had a disproportionate impact upon minority communities. The increased impact on specific communities is apparent using incarceration data following the enactment of specific drug laws. For example, black Americans were incarcerated under crack cocaine prohibition at an alarmingly high rate when compared to other ethnicities.[165] Historically, negative racial sentiments have been used to further the aims of prohibitionists. While today's anti-drug policies lack the explicit racist motivation found in earlier prohibition movements, anti-drug policies are still having disproportionate impact on ethnic minorities. Despite government studies showing similar rates of illicit drug use among most ethnicities[166], intense police enforcement in poor urban areas has resulted in high rates of drug offenses amongst communities of color, even for "decriminalized" drugs such as marijuana.[167]

---

[165] *Trends in Corrections Fact Sheet*, THE SENTENCING PROJECT, 3 http://sentencingproject.org/doc/publications/inc_Trends_in_Corrections_Fact_sh eet.pdf.
[166] 2013 National Survey on Drug Use and Health, http://www.samhsa.gov/data/sites/default/files/NSDUHresultsPDFWHTML2013/ Web/NSDUHresults2013.pdf
[167] New York Times, "Race and Marijuana Arrests." http://www.nytimes.com/2016/11/25/opinion/race-and-marijuana- arrests.html?mabReward=A4&recp=3&action=click&pgtype=Homepage®ion =CColumn&module=Recommendation&src=rechp&WT.nav=RecEngine

V.   Legislative Solutions

The multiple collateral consequences of drug offenses together constitute a substantial barrier to socioeconomic success following conviction for a drug crime. Reducing collateral consequences of drug offenses is possible through legislative solutions, some of which have already been adopted by states across the U.S. Implementing three changes to current laws will drastically reduce the negative collateral consequences that serve as barriers to successful citizen's reentry back into their communities. First, reduce the impact of simple drug possession with the decriminalization of marijuana possession and elimination of first-time felony possession for other drugs. Second, permit statutory expungement for longstanding good behavior. Third, expand economic opportunity by increasing employment discrimination protection for citizens with criminal convictions.

1.   Non-Felony or Decriminalized Simple Drug Possession

Virginia has some of the toughest possession laws in the country, applying misdemeanors for marijuana possession and class 5 felonies for possession of drugs such as cocaine or heroin. The felony possession charges could trigger all the consequences discussed. The collateral consequences of simple drug possession can be reduced while still imposing sanctions on criminalized behavior. Virginia could greatly reduce the damaging long-term impact of punitive prohibition by reducing first or second time simple possession of small doses of heroin or cocaine. For example, West Virginia charges any controlled substance possession with a misdemeanor, and allows for deferment and dismissal for first time offenders.[168] A Three Strike Felony rule could be applied, i.e., classify possession of controlled substances as a misdemeanor offense, but increase punishment incrementally with each subsequent offense with a limit of two misdemeanor offenses before applying a felony. Such a rule would apply a misdemeanor with a mandatory jail time; a second possession offense would be result in another misdemeanor charge, but with significantly increased punishment, such as doubling the time of incarceration. Mandatory substance abuse counseling could also be imposed for all possession charges; ideally, citizens diagnosed as drug addicts could serve out a period of incarceration in supervised, inpatient drug treatment, although this could prove to be costly considering the current healthcare system. Swift and certain punishment will serve as deterrent for potential offenders,

---

[168] W. VA. CODE ANN. § 60A-4-401 (LexisNexis 2016).

but preventing the first-offense application of a felony for drug will decrease the long-term stigma attached to a drug felony if the individual overcomes his addiction and reenters society as a productive member of the community.

Another way to reduce the impact of punitive prohibition on the largest segment of illegal drug users is to decriminalize possession of small amounts of marijuana. Currently, even the misdemeanor charge applied to marijuana, while often carrying little or no actual jail time, still triggers the exclusion from federal educational benefits for a year, the possible eviction from public housing or a private apartment complex for drug-related criminal activity, and suspension of a driver's license. The suspended license also creates the possibility of loss of work, if the conviction alone does not violate the common zero-tolerance policy of many employers.

If the offender is sentenced to jail time, a ten-day sentence in the Commonwealth costs an average of $792.80 to house that inmate.[169] The average daily population of Virginia jails in 2015

---

[169] COMMONWEALTH OF VIRGINIA COMPENSATION BOARD, *FY 2015 Jail Cost Report: Annual Jail Revenues And Expenditures Report (Including Canteen & Other Auxiliary Funds)* III (Nov. 2016) http://www.scb.virginia.gov/docs/fy15jailcostreport.pdf (determining $79.28 was average daily cost to per inmate across regional, local, and farm jails.).

was 29,601; total expenditures to house all of Virginia's inmate population was $979.2 million. Rather than increase the number of inmates for possession, charge marijuana offenders with a civil infraction like a traffic ticket and issue a fine.[170] This will increase revenue, decrease inmate populations, and reduce some of the collateral consequences associated with personal marijuana possession. Decriminalization, or even legalization, allows adults to consume cannabis without the socially crippling consequences of punitive prohibition, and may reduce the stigma associated with the marijuana use to facilitate seeking treatment for those who struggle with marijuana addiction.

2.   <u>Expungement for Longstanding Good Behavior</u>

Another statutory alternative that could significantly enhance the ability for citizens with drug felonies to fully integrate into society would be the expungement of certain nonviolent misdemeanors and felonies after a prescribed time. This would assist individuals sentenced to felonies for simple possession or other non-violent drug offenses to fully overcome their past and move beyond the negative connotations of a drug conviction.

---

[170]*See* DEL. CODE ANN. tit. 16, § 4764 (2016) ("Any person 21 years of age or older who knowingly or intentionally possesses a personal use quantity of . . . [marijuana] . . . shall be assessed a civil penalty of $100 . . .).

Virginia does not offer any statutory expungement for longstanding good behavior, although the General assembly has created a criminal procedure for select expungement "to protect [innocent] persons from the unwarranted damage which may occur as a result of being arrested and convicted."[171] The only expungement available in the Virginia Code is for adjudications that resulted in acquittal or nolle prosequi.[172]

Other states offer criminal records expungement options for people convicted of specific non-violent crimes. Maryland has a much larger list of adjudication results that allow for the expungement of records[173]; effective October 1, 2017, misdemeanants for simple possession of certain controlled substances and alcohol offenses may petition for expungement following 15 years of good behavior.[174] Florida also allows for sealing and expungement of criminal records after ten years.[175] Individuals convicted of misdemeanor drug possession crimes in their youth who are able to overcome such behaviors will not perpetually bear the scar of a drug conviction.

---

[171] VA. CODE ANN. § 19.2-392.2 (2016).
[172] VA. CODE ANN. § 19.2-392.2 (2016).
[173] MD. CODE ANN., CRIM. PROC. §§ 10-102–07 (2016).
[174] MD. CODE ANN., CRIM. PROC. § 10-110 (effective October 1, 2017).
[175] FLA. STAT. ANN §§ 943.0585, 943.059 (LexisNexis 2016).

3.   <u>Prosecution-Free Overdose Reporting</u>

One of the legislative changes that have been instituted by several state legislatures is a concept of "prosecution free" reporting, sometimes referred to as "911 good Samaritan laws. This concept is based in the theory of harm reduction, meaning although people will continue to use drugs, there are steps that can be taken to reduce the harm that drugs have on the individual and the community.

States that have adopted "911 good Samaritan" laws have enacted a variety of bills that shield or reduce criminal and civil culpability for charges relating to the possession of heroin or drug paraphernalia when reporting a drug overdose to save the life of the reporter or another drug user. This is specifically targeted to reduce the rising number of overdose death in America that have been steadily increasing since 1999. From 19999 to 2014, overdose deaths in America have more than doubled. Overdose deaths are the leading cause of injury-related death, surpassing motor vehicle accidents. Many of these increases in overdose deaths has been fueled by the increased use of prescription opioids. Prescription drugs like OxyContin and Vicodin, available at the local pharmacy, accounted for over 18,000 deaths in 2014; in fact, prescription drug deaths outnumbered all illicit drug overdose deaths *combined.* [176]

To combat the rising tide of drug overdose deaths, some states have adopted laws that shield individuals from prosecution for drug charges, in the hope that people will be more inclined to report drug overdoses, even if the drug was not medically prescribed or illegal. For example, Oregon's heroin possession statute uncodified provisions provides any person who contacts emergency medical services or a law enforcement agency to obtain medical assistance for another person or for themselves due to a drug-related overdose is immune from *arrest* or *prosecution* for an offense listed in subsection (3) of this section if the evidence of the offense was obtained because the person contacted emergency medical services or a law enforcement agency."[177] Offenses immune from prosecution include possession of various narcotics, frequenting a place where controlled substances are used, and paraphernalia charges.[178] Additionally, the statute affords similar immunities from parole and probation violations for overdose reporters.

---

[176] Drug Policy Alliance. *911 Good Samaritan Laws: Preventing Overdose Deaths, Saving Lives,* (Feb. 2016).
[177] Or. Rev. Stat. § 475.854 (uncodified provision §§ 1-2) (emphasis added).
[178] *Id.* (uncodified provision §3)

These laws have quickly spread across the country to combat overdose deaths within the several states. New Mexico was the first to pass a "911 good Samaritan" law in 2007; since then, 31 additional states and Washington D.C. have passed similar laws and amendments.[179] A study in Washington showed that 88% of opioid users would be more likely and less afraid to report an overdose after learning about the law.[180] In addition to state-wide statutory changes, over 90 U.S. colleges and universities have enacted drug and alcohol "911 Good Samaritan" regulations for campus police.[181]

4. Needle and Trace Amount Decriminalization

Another legislative solution to reduce the legal impact of heroin is to decriminalize the possession of used heroin needle with only residual, trace amounts of the drug. New York and New Hampshire have put forth legislation that decriminalizes possession of a syringe with a residual amount of drugs.[182] The

---

[179] Drug Policy Alliance. *911 Good Samaritan Laws: Preventing Overdose Deaths, Saving Lives,* (Feb. 2016) (Alabama, Alaska, Arkansas, California, Colorado, Connecticut, Delaware, Florida, Georgia, Hawaii, Illinois, Kentucky, Louisiana, Maryland, Massachusetts, Minnesota, Mississippi, Nevada, New Hampshire, New Jersey, New York, North Carolina, North Dakota, Oregon, Pennsylvania, Rhode Island, Tennessee, Vermont, Washington State, West Virginia, Wisconsin and Washington D.C.).

[180] *Id.*

[181] *Id.*

[182] New York City Bar. "Report on legislation by the committee on HIV/AIDS and the committee on drugs and the law"

purpose of these bills is to allow for clean needle exchange programs, another harm reduction program aimed at reducing the exposure to blood-borne illnesses such as HIV and hepatitis through dirty or shared needles. This legislative change would also prevent over-zealous prosecutors from charging users with heroin possession for the trace amount remaining in the needle.

5.   <u>Second Chance, Ban the Box Legislation</u>

If public benefits are unavailable to low-income citizens returning to the community, the citizen must pursue gainful employment to avoid homelessness and abject poverty. Although Federal law prohibits an explicit, permanent criminal history ban, the ability to turn down applicants based on a business necessity can become a convenient shield to hiring applicants, particularly minority candidates. Virginia could increase the protection for citizens with criminal drug records by adopting more statutory protection for such at-risk or hard to place workers.

First, allow the expungement of criminal records after a certain time, as discussed above. Virginia law currently prevents

---

<http://www2.nycbar.org/pdf/report/uploads/20072925-SyringeDecriminalization.pdf>; Anderson, Dave, "NH Senate to Vote on Needle Exchange Proposal" Apr. 25, 2016 <http://www.fosters.com/article/20160425/NEWS/160429557>.

employers, educational institutions, and state agencies from requesting expunged criminal records.[183] This would allow applicants to avoid discussing convictions from years in the past.

Second, adopt a statutory standard that requires a relation between the conviction and the position or license sought. Currently, Virginia does not have a statutory standard. When considering a criminal record, federal law requires the employer consider the severity of the crime, how long ago the conviction was, the nature of the job sought. [184] New York requires a direct relation between the conviction and the position[185], whereas Kansas law requires the conviction reasonably bear on the applicant's trustworthiness or safety of the business.[186] Clearly establishing the Virginian standard for hiring citizens with criminal records will allow employees to seek positions without fear of elimination based simply upon a nebulous business purpose.

Lastly, Virginia can adopt "ban the box" or "Fair Chance" laws for initial employment applications. When going through a

---

[183] VA. CODE ANN. § 19.2-392.4 (2016).
[184] EEOC Policy Statement on the Issue of Conviction Records under Title VII of the Civil Rights Act of 1964, as amended, 42 U.S.C. § 2000e et seq. (1982) https://www.eeoc.gov/policy/docs/convict1.html.
[185] N.Y. EXEC. LAW § 296(15) (2016); N.Y. CORRECT. LAW §§ 750 to 753 (2016).
[186] KAN. STAT. ANN. § 22-4710(f) (2016).

pile of applications, it is easy to separate those with the "criminal history" box checked off. To prevent such application elimination, Hawaii was the first to enacted Fair Chance laws that remove the criminal history question from private and public employment applications, and required the employers to ask about criminal history following a conditional offer of employment.[187] Illinois first remove the criminal history question from state government applications, and enacted 2013 Illinois House Bill 5701 to adopt the Hawaiian approach.[188] Whether Virginia adopts statutory or administrative changes, allowing applicants a fair chance to compete for gainful employment is an important step in reentering the community as a contributing, tax-paying member.

6.   <u>Drug Court Programs</u>

Another legislative change resulting in positive changes in the judicial handling of drug users has been the creation of Drug Treatment Courts (DTC). In Virginia, the Commonwealth's legislature has enacted the Drug Treatment Court Act.[189] This act allows for the creation of drug treatment court advisory committees, made up of judges, a representative from the

---

[187] HAW. REV. STAT. § 378-2.5 (2016).
[188] 2014 ILL. LAWS 77.
[189] Va. Code § 18.2 – 245.1

commonwealth's attorney, public defenders, and other involved in law enforcement and community supervision. This committee will set the policies and procedures of the court, from the level of collaboration between government entities to selection of participants. Even once selected, the participant must still voluntarily consent to involvement with the program.[190]

Drug courts arose out of the devastation caused by the War on Drugs in America. The 1980's was a time of drug-fueled crime and hysteria which resulted in an overburdened judicial system. Miami was the first to implement a drug treatment court; following its success, drug courts have expanded across the country as an alternative judicial treatment of low-level drug offenders.[191] Some key components to a successful drug court program include:

1. Voice – the ability to participate and voice personal beliefs and opinion has increased satisfaction with process, even if the words had little or no impact on the outcome.

---

[190] Va. Code § 18.2 – 245.1(J)
[191] MacKenzie, Brian. *An AJA White Paper: The Judge Is the Key Component: The Importance of Procedural Fairness in Drug-Treatment Courts*, 52 Court Review 8, 10

2.   Neutrality – ensuring the perception of a neutral arbiter is vital to a satisfactory outcome.

3.   Respectful treatment – although this should be given to everyone as much as possible, it is important to remember to treat addicts with the general respect due any citizen.

4.   Trustworthy Authority – authorities involved with drug court must desire the best outcome for participants, not merely going through procedure to most efficiently expedite the offender to the exit and off to jail. The authorities involved must be committed to success from start to finish.[192]

Of all the authorities involved, positive and constructive interactions with the judge has led to the most positive and successful results. In a survey of participants in an Ohio Drug Treatment Court, 75% said that regular interaction with the judge helped them stay off drugs.[193]

To reach the maximum potential of success, DTC must employ the best addiction treatment models available. One method traditionally employed is narcotics anonymous and analogous

---

[192] *Id.* at 14.
[193] *Id.* at 16.

twelve-step programs. This can be an effective tool with the accountability provided, but only has about a 30% retention rate, normally highly self-motivated individuals.[194] Mental Health Therapy is also regularly used in DTC for avoidance and coping techniques to prevent users from relapsing to drug use or associated behaviors. Lastly, there are medical treatments, such as methadone and extended release naltrexone, which can further assist treatment with addiction to narcotics. DTC should employ all methods available to combat the high levels of dropout from drug court programs across the country, sometime as high as 90% attrition rates.[195]

Graduation or completion of DTC varies, from three months to twelve months, but can last much longer, such as a Virginia DTC in Chesterfield/Colonial Heights, which lasts eighteen to twenty-four months.[196] The process involves more than simply being clean from drugs, but requires a variety of tasks that must be completed, including a variety of treatments and community services.[197] The eligibility requirements for the drug

---

[194] Andraka-Christou, Barbara *Article: Improving Drug Courts Through Medication-Assisted Treatment For Addiction*, 23 Va. J. Soc. Pol'y & L. 179, 185
[195] *Id.* at 201–02.
[196] *Id.;* Rockwell III, Fredrick G., *Essay: The Chesterfield/Colonial Heights Drug Court: A Partnership Between The Criminal Justice System And The Treatment Community*, 43 U. Rich. L. Rev. 5, 8 (2008).
[197] Andraka-Christou, at 204.

court vary, but generally require the person be convicted of a drug crime or associated crime, not have an extensive violent history, live within the jurisdiction, and qualify as a substance dependent person.[198] Once the participant has been identified, at the sole discretion of the prosecutor, the person can choose to be involved. Once involved in DTC, there are a variety of phases that must be completed to successfully graduate from the program.[199] Participants in the Chesterfield DTC graduated at about 40%, and the rest were terminated for failure to comply with the program. Of those graduates, there was a nearly 50% reduction in recidivism; even unsuccessful participants saw a decreased recidivism rate.[200]

7. Jail Diversion Programs

i. *MENTAL ILLNESS AWARENESS*

Today, there are more mentally ill individuals under the care of the criminal justice system rather than mental health facilities that provide treatment.[201] Approximately 16-25% of the national jail population consists of mentally ill individuals who are often

---

[198] Rockwell III, at 13.
[199] *Id.* at 15.
[200] *Id.* at 16.
[201] Leon Evans, *Blueprint for Success: The Bexar County Model*, The Center for Health Care Services, San Antonio, Texas
http://www.fairfaxcounty.gov/policecommission/subcommittees/materials/jail-diversion-toolkit.pdf

incarcerated for simply unusual behavior or non-violent minor crimes. The incarceration of the mentally ill is at an alarming rate, however many officers have very little training in handling mental disease. Deinstitutionalization and a lack of adequate community-based mental health services have caused more persons with mental illness to encounter the criminal justice system, adding to the problem. People with mental illness do not get the help they need in jail, because they are put into an environment that is harmful to treatment and to improving their mental health. Many of these incarcerated mentally ill are homeless and go through a vicious cycle of in and out of jail, through public health facilities, and the street due to inconsistent or inadequate treatment. Then they turn to crime or are imprisoned again for disruptive behaviors.

This problem of incarcerating the mentally ill rather than effectively treating them is not limited to only consumers and their loved ones, but has implications for everyone. There are costs to society and financial burdens shared by the entire community. Some mentally ill frequent parks and streets and join the homeless population, sometimes causing disturbances or suffering dangerous delusions in public places. Significant amounts of police time and resources are used when answering calls for these persons and in waiting 12-14 hours in hospitals for treatment and psychiatric evaluations. Repeated contacts by law enforcement with these same individuals result in increased dollars needed for the criminal justice system, which translate into higher property tax bills for all.

ii.   *JAIL DIVERSION PROGRAM: BEXAR COUNTY MODEL*

It is crucial for the criminal justice and mental health systems to work together to solve the growing mental illness issue; jail diversion programs offer an alternative for judges and prosecutor to redirect the mentally ill away from incarceration and into mental health facilities.[202] The mentally ill can receive treatment through crisis care centers which provide access to immediate care for adults with mental health concerns or substance abuse. Through the program mentally ill patients can also receive support services that help rehabilitate them back into the community.

In Bexar County, Texas, the jail diversion program's goal is to eliminate the inappropriate incarceration of individuals with mental health issues and to reduce the use of arrest and booking process for offenders with mental illness. This program, along

---

[202] *Id.*

with the Crisis Care Center, have been very successful in accomplishing this goal. The Bexar County Program has diverted more than 4,000 individuals with mental illness away from jail and into treatment facilities. The county has experienced enormous savings in millions of dollars annually from a reduction in costs associated with inappropriate jail and emergency room use by the mentally ill. The Crisis Care Center has reduced times that officers used to wait in emergency rooms from 12 hours to 1. The center also has 10 beds and allows individuals to stay up to 23 hours for treatment. The center provides cost effective care outside court system.

Further benefits include reduced emergency room use making more space available to treat other patients, decreased use of jails and prisons allowing room for more violent offenders to be incarcerated, and reduced officer wait times in dropping off consumers which allow officers to return quickly to their duties. A "no-refusal" crisis intervention drop-off center is available for law enforcement and classes are offered to police on mental illness. Mental Health Docket Referrals are another option in place so that those in jail can receive treatment under the supervision of the courts and the Center for Health Care Services. The most important benefit, however, is that the diverted consumers are receiving the help they need regarding treatment and support services.

The program stresses the importance of participation from many groups including: city, county, and state government, law enforcement, the courts, mental health services, hospital facilities, advocacy groups, and consumers. A multitude of intervention points within the community contribute to this program's effectiveness, include as training practitioners, professionals, law enforcement, court officials, and dispatchers to recognizing symptoms and respond appropriately to mental illness, community education, resource sharing, maximum use of pre-and post-trial alternatives, utilizing case managers as court liaisons, and developing advocacy programs to build awareness.

The Bexar County Jail Diversion Program offers integration services of case management, psychiatric rehabilitation, medication access, integrated mental health and substance abuse treatment, life skills training, job placement, peer support, health care, gender-based and trauma-based services, 24-hour confidential crisis line, and links outside services to shelter, food stamps, and insurance that extend care beyond the involvement with the criminal justice system to bring positive change in individual's lives who are effected by mental illness. Treatment plans are developed by case managers at The Center for Health Care Services who are involved. Continuous monitoring of consumers is crucial no matter what facility individuals end up in to ensure they do not "fall through the cracks."

iii. *SETTING UP A JAIL DIVERSION PROGRAM*

Gaining political and financial support for new jail diversion programs can prove to be challenging. Successful programs require participation needed from different groups to advocate for the program and gain outside supporters. Community collaboration and interpersonal relationships that developed through the program are major factors in the success of a jail diversion program. Funding for diversion programs should use every resource available: private donors, charitable organizations, and government assistance. Funding solutions can also include medical partnerships to reduce treatment costs, screening the mentally ill for Medicaid eligibility, and seeking out grants and foundations. Finally, demonstrated success of proven results can help gain support and funding. A newly formed jail diversion program will require some trial and error; the finished product can provide an important mental health treatment asset that could end the repetitive cycle of incarceration for the mentally ill in local

community.

## VI.	Conclusion

For over 100 years, the United States has engineered an extensive policy structure to prohibit and penalize the possession, use, and sale of drugs, historically motivated by racial and subculture prejudice. Today, the collateral consequences of the drug offenses sometimes outweigh the criminal penalty, and serve as a major impediment to the reentry of citizens back into their communities. There are several legislative options that can reduce the collateral effects of drug convictions and allow unimpeded reintegration back into the social and economic fabric of American Communities.

The American War on Drugs continues to take its toll on communities around the country. War-weary law enforcement and illegal drug users have repeated the same hide and seek game, with the stakes often being life or death. There is hope. Cannabis, the most widely used "illegal drug," has lost much of its stigma; states, starting in the western U.S., have ended their prohibition of the plant. Removing the largest subsection of illegal drug users would be a major political windfall, and forever end the exposure to criminal markets for most cannabis consumers.

Despite the change in attitudes towards cannabis, the dangers of synthetic drugs is increased. Opiates use is skyrocketing, leaving a wake of death and destruction. Without change in America's drug policy, the war will continue to rage, and casualties will continue to collect. With results-based solutions and fact-based debates, America can close the chapter of its decades-long War on Drugs and turn a new page in its history by effectively addressing the problem of addiction and substance abuse in the United States.

About the Author

Daniel Rouleau is a 28-year old resident of Virginia Beach, Virginia, married, and father of two sons. He attended the United States Military Academy and Old Dominion University for his undergraduate education, receiving a B.S. in Criminal Justice, and graduated from Regent University School of Law with his J.D. He currently works in public policy/law reform and advocacy, serving as Deputy Director of Virginia NORML, and co-founded Virginia Cannabis Group, Virginia's only cannabis-dedicated government relations and consultant firm. *Half-Truth in Sentencing* is his first non-fiction book. His writing can also be found on several public policy and cannabis-related blogs.

www.ingramcontent.com/pod-product-compliance
Lightning Source LLC
Chambersburg PA
CBHW050843260726
48660CB00006B/2414